Sports Day

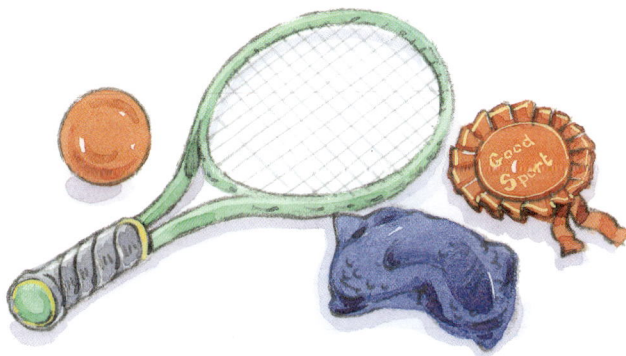

Celia Warren
Illustrated by Shelagh McNicholas

RIGBY

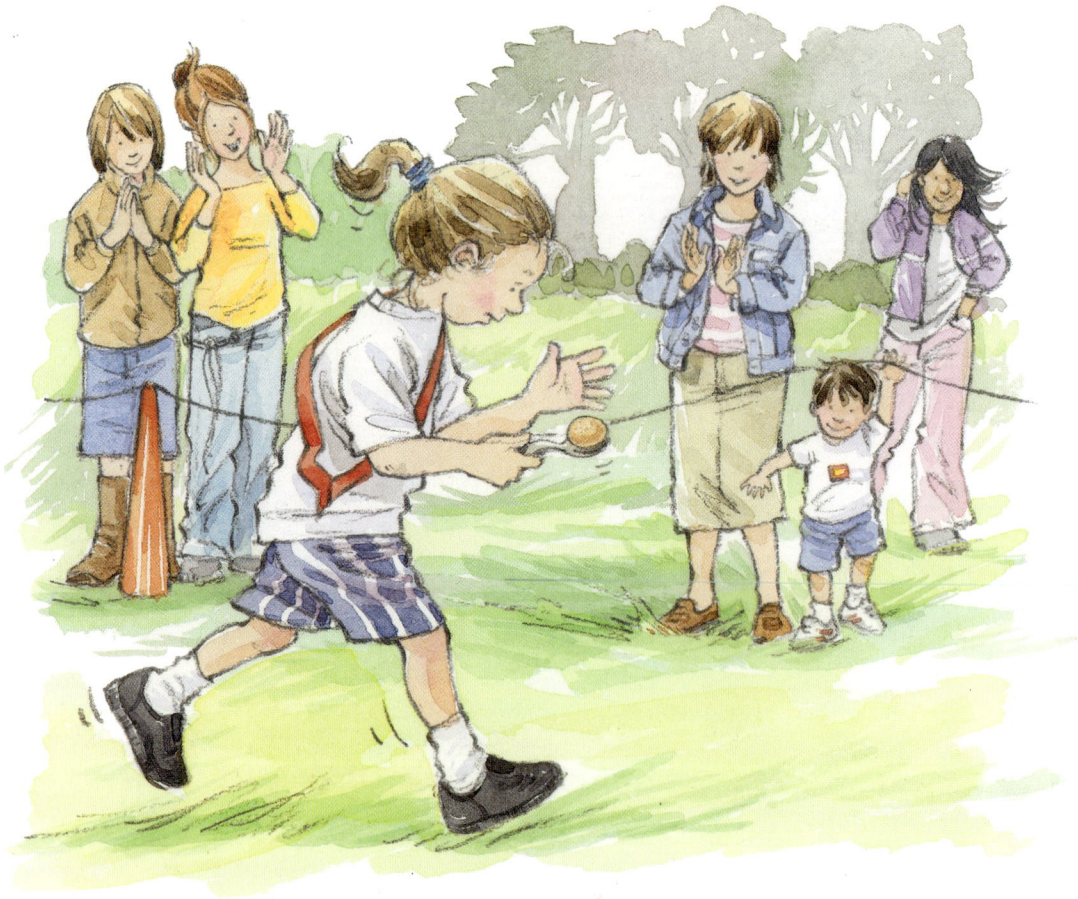

I have an egg and a spoon.

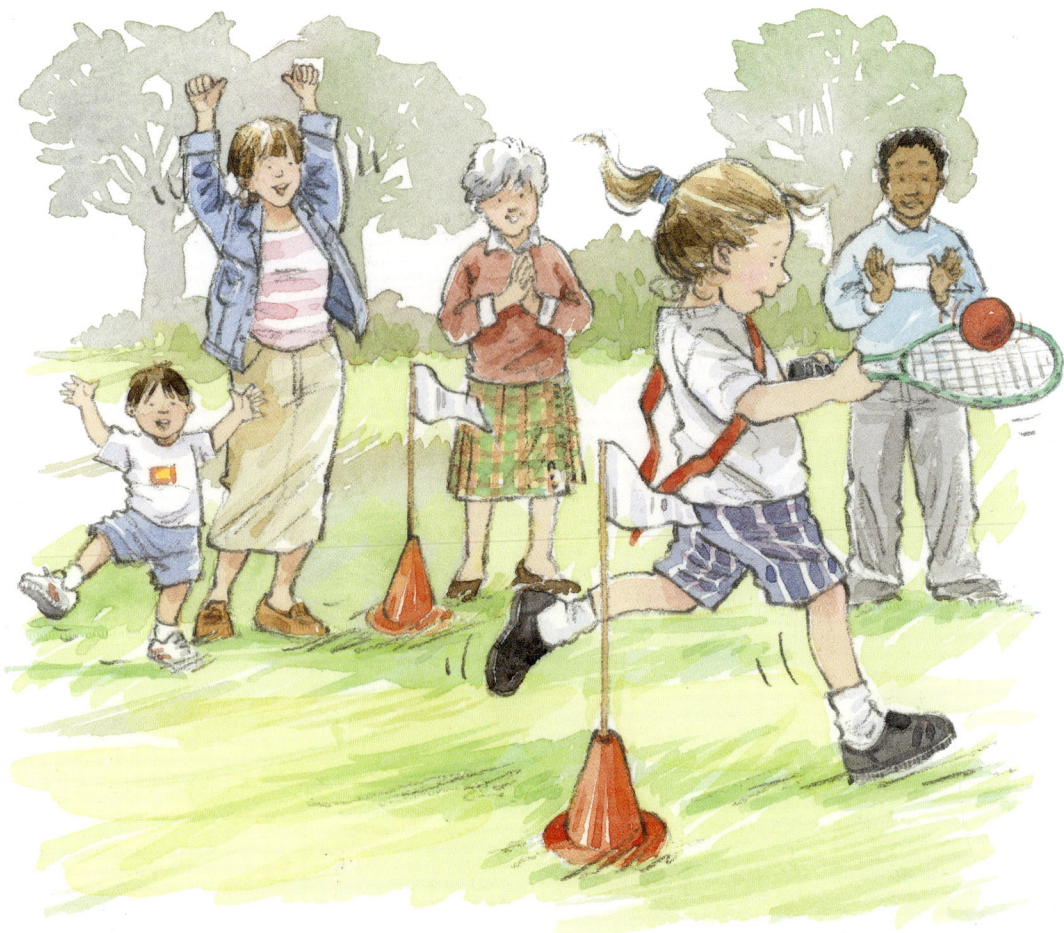

I have a bat and a ball.

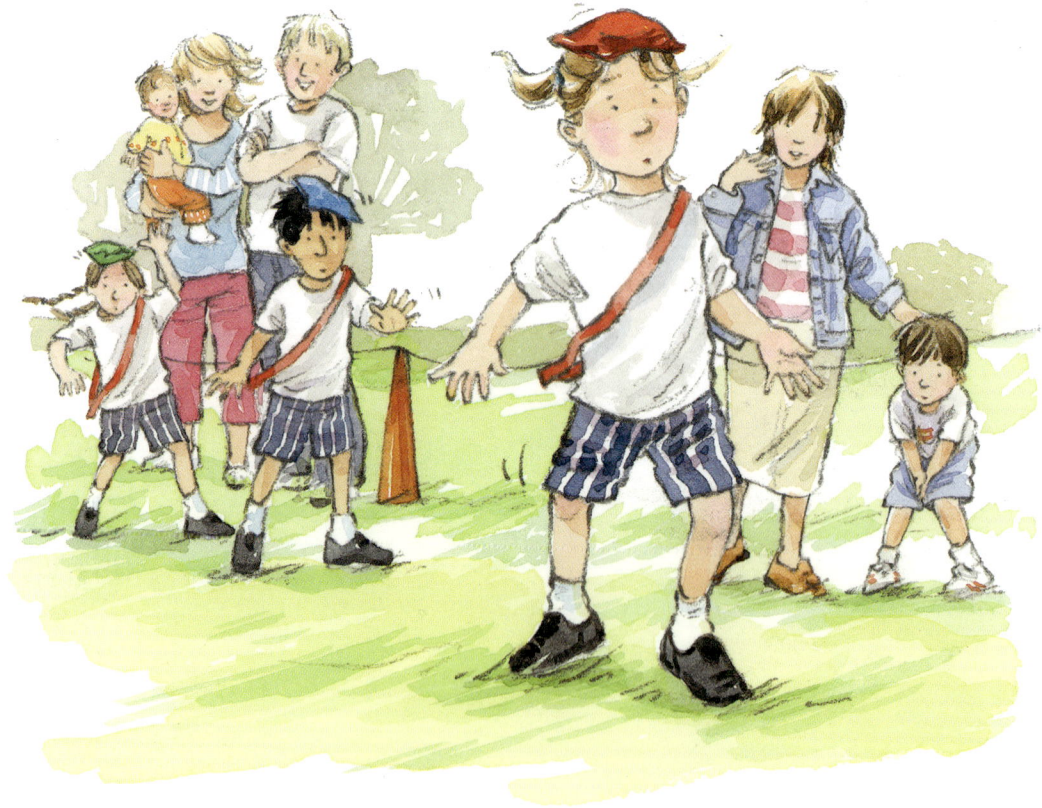

I have a beanbag.

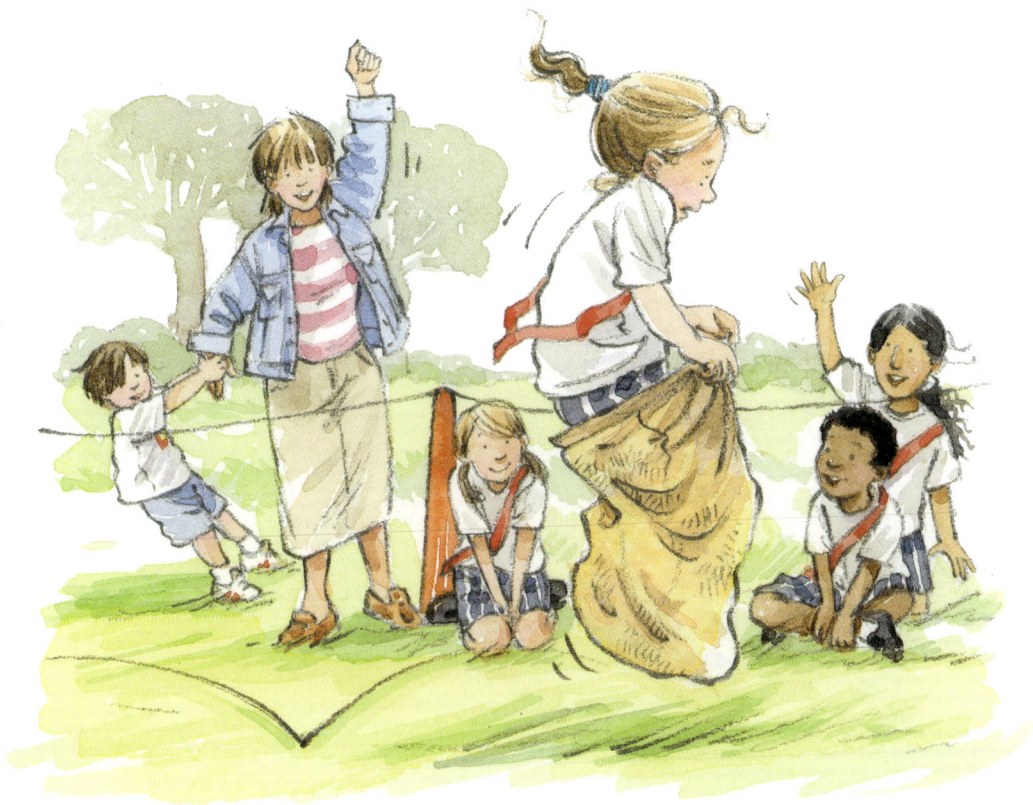

I have a sack.

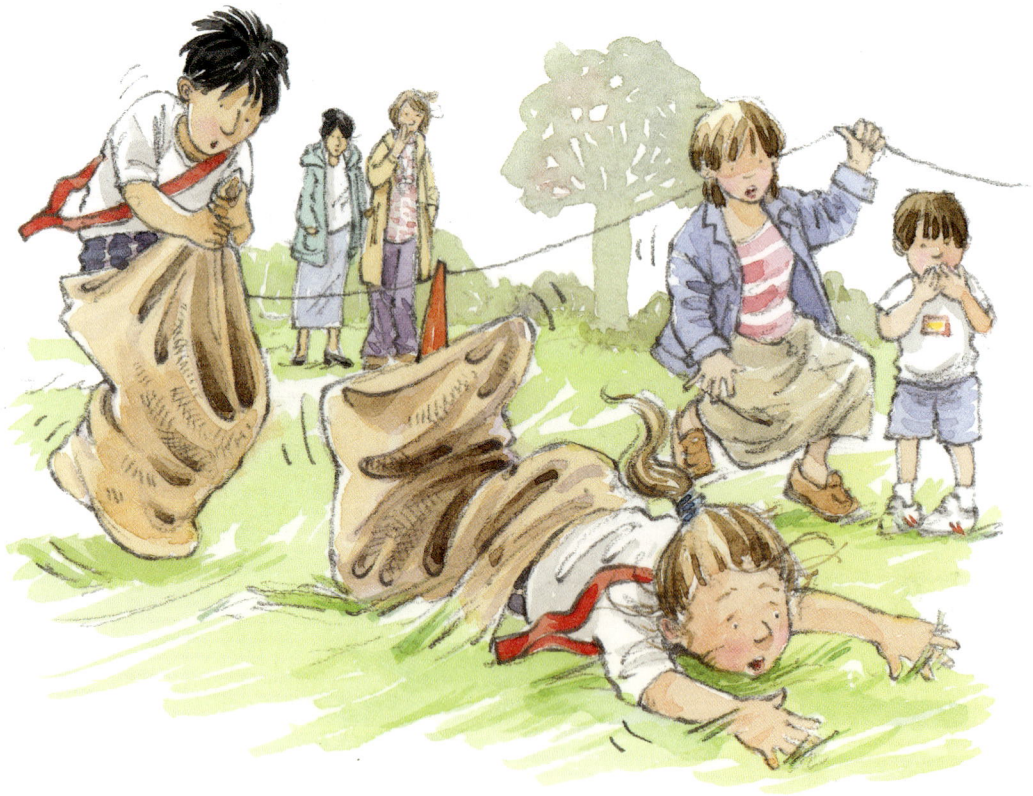

I have a fall.

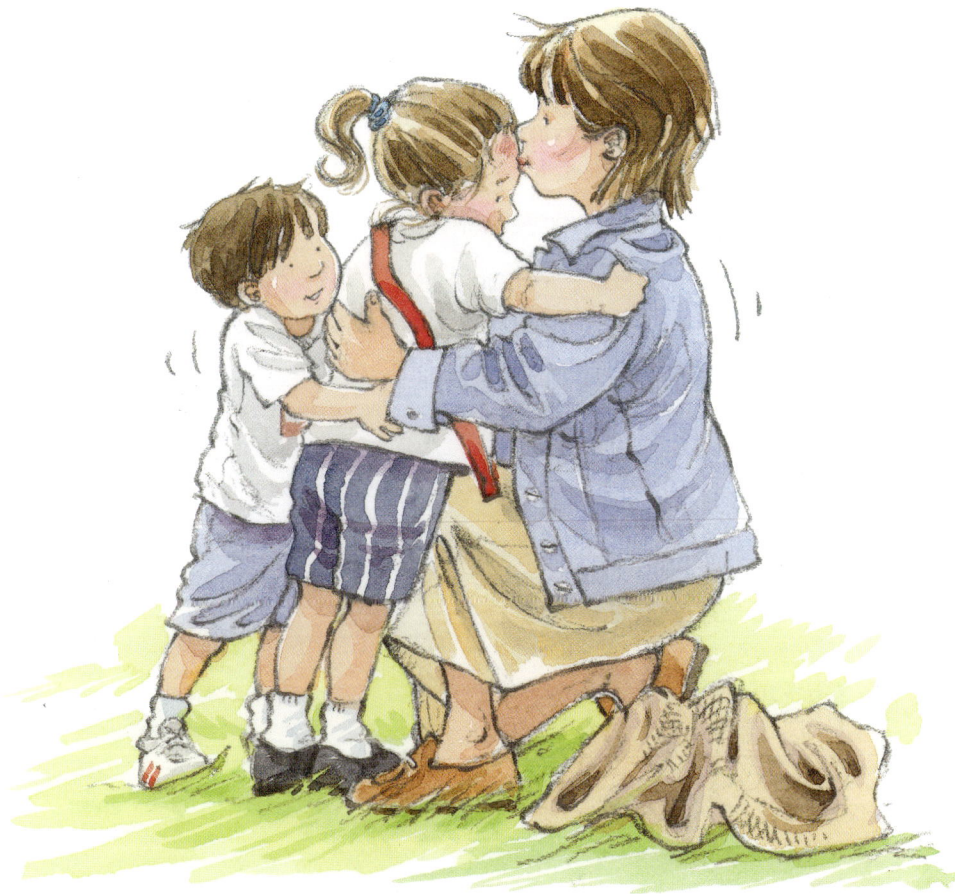

I have a hug and a kiss.

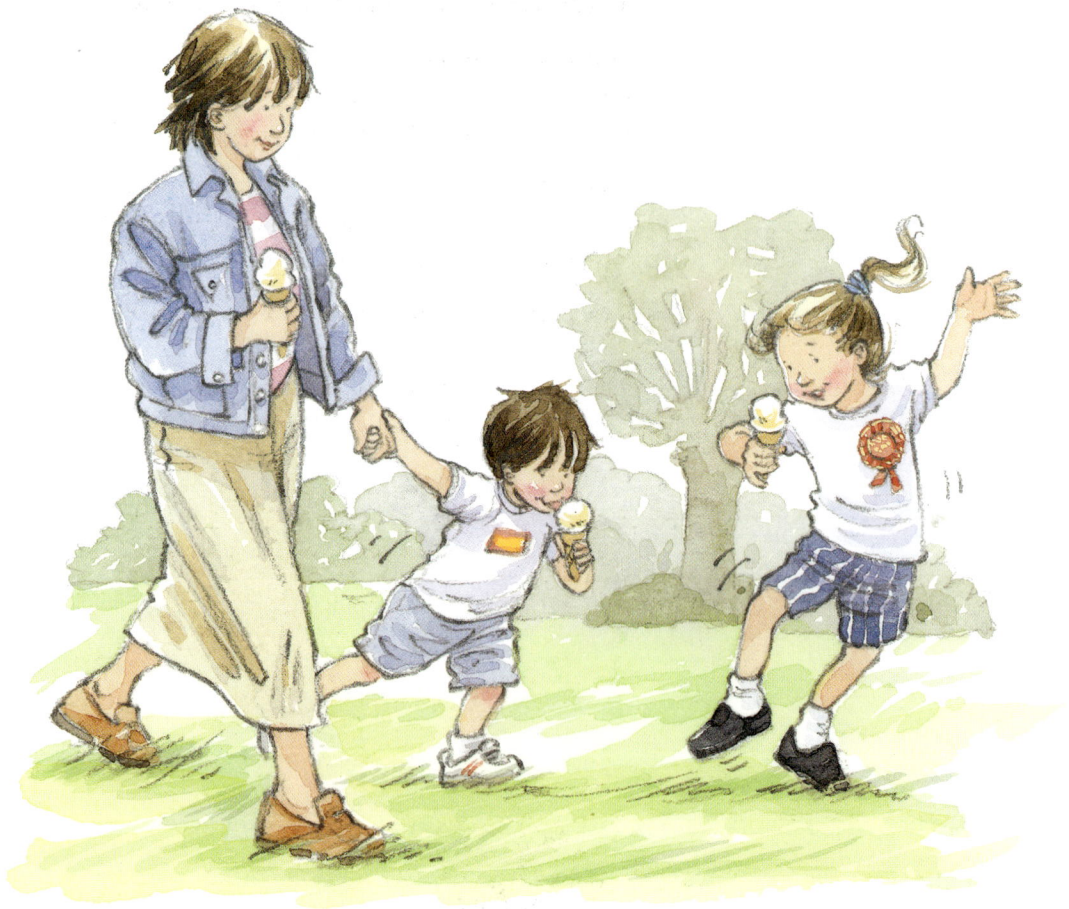

I have a good sports day!